Report on the Second Half of the Twentieth Century

*Report on the Second Half
of the Twentieth Century*
is the thirtieth volume
in the *Essential Poets* Series
published by Guernica Editions.

Ken Norris

Report on the Second Half of the Twentieth Century

Books 1-4

Guernica

Guernica Editions gratefully acknowledge financial support
from the Canada Council.

Guernica Editions, P.O. Box 633, Station N.D.G.,
Montréal (Québec), Canada H4A 3R1.

Legal Deposit — second quarter
Bibliothèque nationale du Québec & National Library of Canada.

Canadian Cataloguing in Publication Data

Norris, Ken, 1951-
Report on the second half of the twentieth century

(Essential poets; 30)
Contents: First report. — The book of fall. — Acts of the imagination.
— Clouds: a sequence of days.
ISBN 0-919349-85-4 (bound).
— ISBN 0-919349-84-6 (pbk.)

I. Title. II. Series.

PS8577.062R46 1987   C811'.54   C87-090035-8
PR9199.3.N67R46 1987

4-23-92

*I do not set down these words, nor did
I compose the poem, out of mere love
of writing. Surely both in China and
Japan art is that which is created when
we are unable to suppress our feelings.*

Ki no Tsurayoki
The Tosa Diary

Preface

These first four books of *Report on the Second Half of the Twentieth Century* were written between February 1976 and June 1980, which now seems like half a lifetime ago. Three of the four books have been published in earlier versions. All four books were revised in 1984 in light of the later books in the series that I was then embarked upon.

I started this "long poem" — this twenty-five year long poem — when I was just turning twenty-five. At the time it seemed to me that T.S. Eliot's *The Waste Land* was a pretty accurate "report" on the first half of the twentieth century. I wrote the first book in the series and called it *Report on the Second Half of the Twentieth Century*, not realizing that it wasn't a complete document. It was, in fact, only the entranceway of a much larger construction.

I thought of that first book as a response to Eliot's vision of a failing civilization. One of the main points I was trying to make was that, if he thought the world was in a sorry state in the post-World War One period, he should catch its act in 1976. The world events of the past ten years haven't done much to change my outlook to a more cheerful one, though where once I saw an impending cataclysm I can now sometimes intuit a possible future for the race and the planet.

Report on the Second Half of the Twentieth Century is my attempt to make a major statement about life in these times. The vantage point is that of the individual life: my own. Collected and juxta-posed, hopefully the books in the series will present a panoramic view and investigation of our moment in history. I've intentionally avoided being stylisti-cally consistent, and the individual books are all structured very differently from the others.

At the time of writing this "Preface," I've written eleven books of *Report* and anticipate writing another eleven before the century's end. At present I conceive of the complete *Report* contain-ing twenty-two books. But who knows? The books get written as they suggest themselves, and I am not writing them with a master plan in mind. Time and events are providing at least as much of the plot and narration as I am.

I'd like to end with an anecdote. In 1970, I took a poetry class with the fine American poet Louis Simpson. One day he managed to reduce the entire class to tears by telling us about Keats, slowly dying of tuberculosis, sitting at the side of an English road spitting up blood. We all cried for that sensitive soul undergoing such pain and suffer-ing. At that same moment thousands of people were starving to death in Bangladesh. We were aware of their suffering, but I doubt that we shed many tears for them. The death of one poet, who had died over a hundred years before, extracted more compassion from us than the suffering of thousands who were dying in our own time. We cried for Keats because he was a great soul; as for the others, their lives were insignificant, hence not deserving of our heartfelt emotions. As George Steiner has pointed out in *Language and Silence*, "There is some evidence that a trained persistent commitment to the life of the printed word, a capacity to identify deeply and critically with imaginary personages or sentiments, diminishes the immediacy, the hard edge of actual circumstance. We come to respond more acutely to literary sorrow than to the misery next door.''

It seems to me that the glory of creation is the life of every individual being. I offer my *Report* in the spirit of that insight.

December 5, 1986
Orono, Maine

1

First Report

HOLY THURSDAY

Is this a holy thing to see,
In a rich and fruitful land,
Babes reduced to misery,
Fed with cold and usurous hand?

Is that trembling cry a song?
Can it be a song of joy?
And so many children poor?
It is a land of poverty!

And their sun does never shine,
And their fields are bleak and bare,
And their ways are fill'd with thorns;
It is eternal winter there.

For where-e'er the sun does shine,
And where-e'er the rain does fall,
Babe can never hunger there,
Nor poverty the mind appall.

William Blake
Songs of Experience

I

The Waste Land was only a beginning:

Now even the third generation sores
Are beginning to fester.
At the four corners people stand
Wailing for their supper.

All fragments have sub-divided.
Bulldozers clear the human trash heaps.

Missiles in their silos,
Waiting.

This is what happens when cells
Don't regenerate. Total breakdown.

What Love has become only
Psychology can say. As for Beauty,
She was killed in the form of a deer
Trying to cross the turnpike.

☐

Born
In April '51, child
Of the second half.
Like a hooked fish
They pulled me from the waters
Of stillness and sleep.

Early on the convulsions began, my eyes rolling up.
They would shove a bottle of vinegar under my

13

nose to bring my eyes down. I did not want to look. They placed me in my crib, dressed in blue pajamas. I sucked on the big toe of my left foot. I tried to ignore the world.

☐

PSYCHIC CAN bewitch (mesmerize) loved ones, others to do your bidding. Write requests. Donations appreciated.

☐

In 1929 American businessmen
Took to jumping out
Of windows. I know
It is ancient history.
Now they wear the latest
Fashions and try to pretend
Nothing has happened.

The sky goes white with fear so often
Everyone begins not to notice.

At some point
Something went wrong. I would
Pin it on Descartes.

☐

QUEBEC (CP) — A 53-year-old woman was killed yesterday when she was hit by a CNR freight train at the nearby community of St. Jean de Chrysostome. Police said Mrs. Rodolphe Roberge was walking along the train tracks and apparently failed to hear the oncoming freight.

□

Someone may write someday of how I walked around in my middle twenties feeling slightly deranged. If there is paper left. If I have made some mark. If anyone can still read.

For years the United States did not recognize the existence of Red China, though they would have been hard pressed to prove to anyone that it wasn't there. We refuse to recognize the hungry, the weak and the dying. If a history remains, this century will go down in it as the cruelest time of all. For mass genocides, yes, but above all because we knew of all the terror and human suffering. We sat in our living rooms watching it all on tv, then turned it off and did nothing.

□

WASHINGTON — (CP-UPI) — A large earth fracture known as the Motagua Fault has been blamed for the earthquake that hit Guatemala last week, the U.S. Geological Survey reported today. Government geologists who surveyed the scene said the fault runs east-west from a point about 15 miles north of Guatemala City eastward probably as far as Puerto Barrios near the Gulf of Honduras. It had been recognized earlier as a potential cause of earthquakes. The Guatemalan government reports that 18,901 people died in the earthquake and the aftershocks that rocked the country over the last week. It listed 62,432 injured and more than one million homeless.

□

I have begun again
To collect evidence.
Of God's absence from the world.
Of man's inhumanity to man.

☐

OTTAWA — (CP) — Despite the fact that a doctor's survey
has uncovered symptoms of mercury poisoning among Que-
bec Indians, Health Minister Marc Lalonde said yesterday
there is no need for panic.

He was replying in the Commons to Stuart Leggatt
(NDP-New Westminster), who mentioned the survey con-
ducted earlier this year.

Leggatt said the study uncovered symptoms of mer-
cury poisoning among 23 of a group of 40 Indians. Three of
them were shown to have suffered brain damage.

The British Columbia MP asked whether the govern-
ment is looking into alternate sources of protein to get the
Indians off their fish-based diet, which is the problem in the
Grassy Narrows and White Dog reserves in Ontario, where
so-called Minamata disease has been discovered.

The fish absorb mercury from lake and river water and
when consumed by human beings, the metal attacks major
organs and the nervous system, sometimes fatally. It first
was found in Minamata, Japan.

Lalonde said the federal government is in "very close
consultation" with the Quebec government over the latest
discoveries. But he suggested there was no need for wide-
spread concern because these were isolated cases.

☐

You've seen one atrocity
You've seen them all.

I especially enjoyed
The Vietnam War.

□

According to Woodward and Bernstein's upcoming book, *The Final Days*, David Eisenhower became so concerned about his father-in-law's mental health in the summer of '74 that he called Sen. Robert Griffin (R-Mich) and asked him to urge Nixon to resign. Apparently Nixon had taken to saying good night to all the portraits of former presidents hanging on the second floor of the White House.

Eisenhower and Edward Cox are two thinly disguised sources for the book (for which NEWSWEEK reportedly paid six figures for first-serial rights). Julie Eisenhower has already denied the story, adding that there are nothing but landscapes on the second floor of the White House.

□

Each time I fall from Grace
I have to borrow the neighbor's
Stilts to get back up. Seriously
Though, Dante's *Inferno* is selling
At Cheap Thrills for 49¢.

Religion aside, God's been on vacation
For the last 300 years.
One day he got tired of listening
To the umpteenth boring confession
And lit out for the other end of the universe.
I still worship him from afar.

□

STONY BROOK, L.I. Feb. 21 — When Kofi Awoonor packed to go home to Ghana, there were the textbooks for the college library back home, and the seeds for his brother's farm. It was not the luggage of a man going home to cause trouble, his friend, Steve Becker says.

But now Mr. Becker's friend is in serious trouble in Ghana, West Africa. Mr. Awoonor, a poet and teacher of international stature, was arrested on Dec. 21, amid rumors of a possible coup, and has been held incommunicado ever since. His colleagues are mounting a campaign to help him, but are frustrated by how little they can do for a friend imprisoned in his homeland.

"Kofi is not a political man," says Mr. Becker, who was a student of Mr. Awoonor at the State University of Stony Brook. "I never heard him make remarks about going home for political causes, or show feelings against his government. They invited him back to teach."

☐

Endre, we have been wrong
In thinking poetry and politics
Make for a heavy-handed marriage,
That there is a thin wire
We must walk when trying to bring
Politics into the poem.
It is impossible to keep politics
Out of the poem.
Too often we hang back at the borders
Where our silence means assent.
To remain quiet is to do nothing, to be
An involved witness who, unknowingly,
Helps to prosecute the case against himself.

☐

It is never too late to change
But we are losing the will to change.

If we are not bearing witness
To the cruelties of the human heart
We, ourselves, are perpetrating
A reign of cruelty upon others.

We have driven a stake
Through the heart
Of the word *compassion*.

☐

GOVERNMENT OFFICIALS IN ACCRA
REFUSE TO CITE THE CHARGES
AGAINST KOFI AWOONOR

ACCRA, Ghana, Feb. 24 (AP) — Government officials have confirmed the arrest and detention of Dr. Kofi Awoonor, a Ghanaan novelist and poet who has taught at the State University of New York in Stony Brook, L.I.

The officials refused to cite charges or elaborate on the case on grounds that investigations were still in progress. They said no one was ever detained without cause.

II

When Ezra Pound got out of St. Elizabeth's, the first thing he did was go to a Chinese restaurant in Washington, D.C. and order chicken chow mein. The spirit of Confucius lingered in the bean sprouts. Thank you, George Bowering, for telling me such a delightful story that is, in every part, true. I want nothing false to become part of this account.

When a friend pointed out to Freud that, with his penchant for cigars, he was circling his mouth around quite a phallic symbol, Freud remarked that sometimes a cigar is only a cigar. Freud smoked cigars in the first half of the twentieth century; Pound committed his crimes during that same span of 50 years, and it was a new age when he finally left St. Elizabeth's, though the world could still offer him chicken chow mein.

Last night, after your reading, Endre, Carol and I ordered chicken chow mein, while you, George, sat smoking a cigar, not eating chicken chow mein but won ton soup. The restaurant we were in was not on the Main but on narrow La Gauchetière. In Canada, you said, history is writing history. Exactly; I am writing history. It is history in the making, often out of the main of what historians will choose to put in textbooks, but still on the table: residue in the bottom of a chinese tea cup.

□

In dreams begin responsibilities.

W.B. Yeats

Sweet Dreams. Too often in blissed-out-junkie-sleep I dreamed the dream of the thousand-petalled lotus flower, each member of the human race unfolding like that flower. Flower Power.

Don't underestimate what Woodstock was: the fruition of 2,000 years of difficult loving. Dreamers All.

Wise sage Tiresias dreamed nothing, saw nothing but what was: Oedipus in the sack with mother, the tawdry affair of girl with gramophone, sadnesses of the day. Lewd Realities.

I stood on a street corner at high noon, dreamed the moon came up, and it did. In the realm of human possibilities, love sprouted like a seed in my aerated brain.

☐

Rest easy, T.S. Eliot, this poem dies with each line I write. Your memory remains. On the wrong side of a crack-up you envisioned a Waste Land, had Ezra Pound to tighten it up. I hold now to sanity and declare everything to be worse. There are no cup and lance powerful enough to renew this world. Thunder does not speak to us. Snow is falling on the carefully placed chess pieces. The missiles are aimed and armed.

III

Slowly the world slips away;
I am back in my study, self-involved.
When snow falls it covers the world
Like a shroud and we sleep.
I close my eyes. When
The world is buried I no longer
Feel the need to mourn it. Let
It rest in peace. Only when
I see it clearly in its agony
Do I want to cry out in its defense.

□

Though I try to find engagement with the world I don't know it, have left this continent only once; went to Europe to get my seasoning. Met a girl named Hope in a park on the Left Bank, stood with her on the steps of Montmartre looking down onto Paris at night, saw the lights and found a quick connection to the source that kindles romance.

Yet I could not get out of Germany fast enough. What was there? Roots leading me down into the past, the dark cellar of the century. In America I had seen a movie showing what the Allies found when they crashed into the death camps of Germany in 1945. A film crew recorded images, the naked truth: bodies piled high in mounds of rotting flesh. That was the European fact I could not escape.

□

Invoking words, I tax
The scope of my vision.
What do I see? Pynchon's entropy.
I will not inhabit the hothouse
In order to see things grow.

Lately, whenever I look
In the mirror, I see Marcel Duchamp
Playing that endless chess game.

□

Capitalism is a wheel
Rolling over the breadth of our bodies,
In its lust rolling
Too fast to stop.

I can only forgive the unknowing.

☐

Was she Beautiful? For she was definitely the
contemporary woman, her name V., and where has
Beauty gone, how many ways transformed? Every-
one admitted she made them think of fucking,
even the women. I would not say she was beautiful,
but she made *me* think of fucking, and often she
talked of whips and chains.

IV

Silence means assent.
        So I go on talking, try to filibuster the present
policies, in so doing only cancel out my life's
actions, perhaps, in that way, do some good. Every
day I don't go off to work I undermine the system.
I really believe that. Those days I not only say no, I
do no.

☐

To write about myself
Is to write about the age.
This poem is not lost;
It is finding itself in me.

I am writing it
The same way
These 50 years
Are writing me.

□

While at the age of six
I sat in grandmother's bedroom
Playing with inanimate stuffed toys,
Pretending to give them life,
One of my heroes, Malcolm Lowry,
Was choking to death
On his own vomit
In his bedroom in Sussex, England.

Years later, on mescaline, I saw
The long shadow and the dark abyss
Fall at my feet, but the Mexican
In the unlighted corner of my soul
Did not push hard enough and
All around me the mongrel dogs were barking.

February 13-April 3, 1976
Montreal

2

The Book of Fall

True poetry is born out of the very despair that the word is useless and poetry is to be abandoned.

Shinkichi Takahashi

History
is over, we take place
in a season...

Margaret Atwood
"Book of Ancestors"

Tonight rain's falling
and television news
reports Presley dead at 42;

Along roadsides
I have already seen the foliage
of older trees beginning to turn,
and in the forest isolate scarlet
maple leaves have achieved
their fullness in life
and dropped to the ground.

☐

The hard lines of the outer
encasing the soft dark broken lines within.

Arriving at St. Johnsbury before 10 in the morning,
we've got 6 hours to kill before boarding the bus at
4:25 for Portland, going to the sea. So Barbara and
I buy our bus tickets, dropping off my pack and her
travel bag, then walk the narrow streets to check
the limits of the town. When rain starts falling we
duck into the National Science Museum, walk
around its first floor looking into glass cases at taxi-
dermied birds, study them trying to glean some
knowledge. I linger at the cases filled with hum-
mingbirds: birds indigenous only to this new
world, strange birds out of tropical forests.

When the rain stops we go outside to see the
live museum in back where we find owls tied to
trees with ropes — one of them knowingly winks at
Barbara — and a caged raven who brashly caws ''I
love school!'' in an almost human voice.

Later, on the bus, travelling through New Hampshire, the road is flanked by high green mountains, the road hemmed in with only a narrow trail to follow, my vision hemmed in, restricted to rows upon rows of green trees and mountains so high, their trails so steep, coming into my vision now: the things I can't cope with, the mountains I cannot climb.

In Portland, the sky afire with red, we hunt out a hotel room; we wind up at the Eastland Motor Hotel on High Street. In the room the tv is on the fritz, only two stations to be had, a few of the lights don't work, and so I start looking for something to steal.

Hungry, we wander out into the streets of Portland, find almost everything closed, pass a movie theatre where there is (oddly) an Elvis Presley film festival on, and generally marvel at how dead a town Portland is, shut down and almost locked up tight at 9:30.

Finally winding up in a pizza joint called The Yellow Submarine, we order a pie and wait for the guy who makes them to return. When he comes back he makes us a mushroom and garlic pizza; we devour it (haven't had anything to eat since 1 and now it's half past 10); then, eavesdropping on his conversation with a friend who has come in, we hear the pizza man say he's going to be on tv that night, talking about the effect the cancelled Elvis concerts are going to have on business along Congress St. (Portland's main drag), come to realize Elvis was due to open his national tour in Portland this very night.

Back at the hotel I put on the news while Barbara takes a shower. I don't see the pizza man but instead the overweight female owner of Recordland talking about how, when she opened the store that morning, there were 50 people waiting to get in, and how they came in and picked up stacks of all of Elvis' records, cleaning her out, and how she could have sold many more if only she'd had them.

☐

Barbara lying on her side under the blankets here in our room, reading *Healing Ourselves*, I am left with only the literal facts, small acts of doing, mind bereft of any imaginative consciousness. The ocean has poured out at my feet a thousand times and been only water, and, pulling back each time in undertow, has left me completely with what I had, has taken nothing, given nothing but a view of tides running in and out,

    light falling upon the bluegreen water,
    the absolute reality of the sea.

    And I dreamed last night that I was Louis Dudek's adopted son, and became angry when he did not treat me in a fatherly way, and though I cannot remember the identity of my mother in that dream, I remember she begged me to try and understand him. One day I received two postcards from him and the first said "I am dying, son, and will be leaving your mother in a state of debt, and you must take care of her." And the moment's strange gratification of being recognized as a son was undercut by the postcard's salutation which read "Cordially, Louis Dudek." I woke up before ever reading the second card, it was early morning, Barbara was also awake and she said "Look out the window." I got out of bed and saw the sun 15 minutes out of the sea, and the clouds in the sky all pink and yellow, light reflecting off the water.

Now, as Barbara sleeps, having dropped off in the middle of her reading, I think about my own father, never having accepted him, at the same time inwardly hurt and disappointed that he has never truly shown me any fatherly affection, but only acted like a man trying to reel in a fish; the fish is as stubborn as the man, and the fight will continue forever, for neither of them will give up, show pity, or cry.

A while ago I thought "If I am dying there is so much I have to come to terms with," and I thought of my parents and how my relationships with them need straightening out: how I would have to learn to let my mother near me again, and how I would have to learn to love my father for the very first time. There would also be the loves of my life that came apart; I would have to make my peace with those ladies before I could die, or else I would die in a state of incompleteness, with nothing achieved, all my life lines cut. I became resolved about working it all out until I knew I was still firmly rooted in life; then my resolve slid away, all the people in my life are still kept strangers.

The reality the sea brings
on the silver tray of its waves
breaking against the shore, depositing
silt, wearing away the coastline, moving

in and out with the regularity of tides:
my feelings, the constant ebb and rise
of my life, the burden of them
constantly at work beneath
the blue elevation of the transcendental sky.

☐

Small impressions
striking flint in my head,
sparking small fires; small fires
burning a short time, producing little heat.
Urgency is not in the words
but in the impulse behind them,
the need to articulate in speech
my passing days, my life burning out
like a star, beautiful in its fashion
though scarred by the wounds of attitude
and past expression; the need is for
the acceptance of failure.

☐

This morning's rainfall
puts me back in her arms,
wrestling with the protean
forms she became, unnaturalness
at the heart
of her transformations.

☐

Given time
and a book of blank pages to fill

and a season unfolding
all around my senses
I struggle on,
grappling with words and my own tired eyes,
my even-tempered eyes that see extinction
sweeping the air and earth with a broom,
not having found connection to the wise heart
that has resolved the difficulties
of seeing, still
amidst the change, staying
one constant color, the color of compassion,
as all of nature changes hue.
The world is ever beautiful;
even the scars on her belly
are marks of love.

☐

I wonder where I started from,
what dark spark
fired this fuel to flame?
I tell you, when day breaks
I am in pain, rolling over
inside dreams across a landscape
that resists me. Over my
left shoulder I see it, full moon,
wildnesses I can't tame,
shadowy animal, but real to me,
real, so evidently there.

☐

When the moon speaks
I listen, back tensed,
my stomach not a center for the sun,

my mind a cavity, a crater
filling up with borrowed light.

☐

Unable to push past
the dropped screen.
When words desert me
I am abandoned to
a night of cold and loneliness,
the awful truth,
the distance we stand at
so far from any station.

☐

Day broke before I opened my eyes, caught in a
dream in which a friend counselled of how the
spirit is lost when one stays too long away from the
life one is born to. And his advice was swept away
by the sudden appearance of a blonde-haired girl I
know lying in my bed, wearing her glasses and
reading, her life somehow twinned with mine.

And when I awoke Barbara said she'd had a
lovely dream in which I was 15 years older but smil-
ing and laughing, and that we had a five year old
blonde-haired daughter who was obviously the
lamp that was lighting up my life.

Later, Willy at the Print Shop said he'd had a
dream the night before in which he'd gotten mar-
ried, and the bride turned out to be a friend of his
mother's, and on the eve of their wedding night
she suddenly was dead, though, in actuality, she'd
already been dead a year.

□

Branches break in the wind,
the snap of their separation
a definite sound, a sound
I know at root center,
the snapping off
and tumbling to the ground
a life process, the way nature
begins to sweep itself clean.

□

Yes, yes, I know that,
a woman's voice finding utterance
inside my head, the voice
of the other side.

□

Settling into the night
with a girl's blonde hair
becoming the tangled web
of memory. It's so dark,
don't know if I mean
inside or out; the inner darkness
never abates, the sewer you
kicked open still yawns wide.
What I am writing about
is how it all comes apart,
how nature in pieces is nothing,
lacks the vital drive at its center
that, in spring, forces the flower out.

□

What we know of fall
is that it is beautiful
and it is the beauty
         of stripping away.

□

The truth of our lives is that we fail.
To love. To make our testimony
in the face of impermanent nature.
Immortality goes against the grain
of everything we know. Yet we strive
for it and, in striving, fail,
toss ourselves onto the pyre of language,
burn for a time, but never burn clean.
To bare the self
to the abuses of what is
begins a process, the coming to know
one is incapable.
There is nothing
new in this, though
we have uncovered the furrow
of the little we truly know.

□

The reality is rain
as it pours out
into this life.
To be denied sunlight shimmering
in the autumn leaves

is to be deprived of
        all grace.

In my life
cloud cover
and so many days rain
there is no sense left
        to be made.

I wanted to be able to say
we are beautiful, graceful;
when we are still and bathed in light
there is nothing more perfect,
not even the trees, for when
grace illumines the human face with light
I understand why painters
clung for so long to the human form,
why Rembrandt painted portraits
and left landscape for the mere technicians.

And the trees?
They tenaciously endure.

I wanted to say that fall
is a picture of how we die
if only we understand what is dying
and what remains behind, in the world,
the world into which
we are now incorporated,
becoming humus, becoming air.

Rain destroys the merry aesthetic
that cries out against fall, drowns
all beauty, all capability for it.

And I feel a fool, talking about beauty,
hearing the falseness of that word echo,
knowing it is something else I reach for,
something we have accepted
the word *beauty* be tied to but which
is not that, is like
an annunciation, a real beginning
to something breaking into the world
which we can only stand in awe of.
And what we stand in awe of is light.

An open window provides
a sudden clarity, cold breeze
blowing into the room, bare tree
stark against the almost white
mid-morning sky. That tree has been
stripped clean, stands like clear thought,
the outline of its branches so definite, so sure.

I hear myself say
"How long can I continue
to think about
one action,
of trees, the transformation
in the color of leaves,
their ripping from the bough and
falling to the ground;
how long can I
keep looking at trees
and see myself?"

I can. I do.
It is all
contained in that.

□

You have to picture
a man turning the pages of a book,
finding so many pages blank
and feeling a compulsion to fill them
with small parts of himself,
tiny morsels of his inner being.
As if that small act of grace
could soften the blow
of so much empty space,
as if words could become worlds
that he could live in and thereby
avoid being lonely.

Seeing a white page I am, at times,
like a bull seeing red.
I have no choice
but to rush ahead,
though I find myself
lost in a dance that seems endless,
cheered for its futility
by the angels in the arena
who admire the brilliant moves
of the matador; and still
I see before me
all I must destroy, and guised
behind that, undoubtedly, is held
the blade with which I am to be flayed.

□

The sun beams with a renewed force, as if, now that everything has been decided, it can assert itself again. I wake up to find myself out from under the influence of Scorpio, now floating softly, becalmed. The rough passage is over, the agony of seeing the natural world in its final stage of mutilation dissipated, leaving behind a clear blue sky lined with white clouds and the beautiful skeletal structure of bushes and trees.

And to push the metaphor a little further, that stark bare tree that I see across the street every morning upon waking and looking out the bedroom window, that tree is surely myself. It is like the language stripped of its colors, with only a skeletal toughness that is its final perfection, as it is mine.

The magic of trees: to be beautiful when it is their time to be beautiful, to be stark when naked truth is required. And then to shoot out powerful buds in spring, to start the process over, renewed, in a way miraculous, something the human form cannot do: go down to bone and then come back with a new flesh; only in the mind do we change, rediscovering old senses. But the tree is ever itself, full of consciousness, knowing its loss of beauty and not caring, perfectly engaged and disengaged with the world in which it's rooted.

[ ]

I was talking to Auden, and he was telling me that the poem he considered his finest achievement had never been published, whereupon he began to recite it to me in his clear accented voice. It was a poem about twelve lines long, incredibly simple, and when he had finished reciting it I told him it sounded good, but I wasn't sure it was the best thing he had ever written, even though the last lines were still echoing in my mind. So he recited it again, and the poem moved along with the same simple grace, and I thought if only I could remember it I could write it down and call it my own. But the poem moved along and, after it was over, I found I couldn't remember even a single line of it.

☐

Pure helplessness in the face of Barbara's high fever, and no other symptoms showing, whatever she has a mystery. I stand outside of it, worrying, angry that, at times like this, there is nothing we can do for the ones we love, nothing we can do to take their pain away, nothing we can do to save them.

An hour ago I stood by the window, watching sparrows fly over snow-drenched trees in precise bomber patterns, snow falling everywhere, piling up outside the window; I was caught in the feeling of loss, not thinking that this is, in any way, a mysterious ailment that claims her, but feeling the situation as it could be; and myself, in a moment of pure terror, feeling an incredible loneliness, and that loneliness affirming the reality of my love.

☐

Returning to the arms of the love poem
I find you here
waiting for me.
Are we to begin again, the sun
so bright, melting the snow,
our bedroom a veritable garden?

Working my way out of loneliness,
the dark negative space where everything dies,
I find you, the only flower
that continues to blossom in winter,
that blossoms daily, the wonder
and process of that action
totally unknown to you.
Someone with a camera for truth
would find you huddled under covers,
a little worse for wear, your hair
uncombed, thumbing through a magazine.
You call out to me, I run to you;
you are sitting in the sunlight
getting frustrated, trying to read a book
about, of all things, freemasonry.

□

The biggest storm of the year
they say, and to me it's only mist.
Snow is pelting the city
with the insistence of memories,
and I have been remembering
the bodies, the hands
of women who came wrapped
in transparency, so apparent,
parading through my apartment,

riding up the 14 floors by elevator
to lie down and lash out against dying
in the act of sex, only to
depart again, enter into
the black void where memory ends;
their lives approach
to carry them off to some greater darkness,
or through magical routine
out into the real light of day.

◻

One day this life will be memories,
this apartment a place I lived with you,
and you will be gone
or else in the kitchen with an apron on
and it will be the future
we never prepared ourselves for.

◻

From here on
it's a cold road,
a loveless dance
through the snow,

what I see with my eyes,
extend my hands and fit into,
a space not empty
but full to the brim
with something so pure
I cannot tolerate it.

◻

The irony of winter closing in,
padlocking the windows that lead
to that beautiful outer world.

I thought I just caught
a glimpse of a woman
or else just felt the muse
entering my mind, becoming
the generator of words
I hardly know the meaning of.
I am tiring of words
as early rising children
must tire of the night.

□

The touch-tone phone of December lies beneath
my hands, offers the promise of connection, a
direct call placed to anyone on this dark night; I
could call my shadow or the spirits that used to
haunt me, that I miss in the late hours; they will
accept the call without question. I can call anyone
and they will answer (that's the proposition).

   I call you and ask if you still love me. Why no,
you say, in fact I haven't even thought of you in 7
years, I'd forgotten you totally until you called. It's
only been 5, I say, choked up with time and an
excess of sentiment. Yes, well, I was already prac-
ticing at the time we met, you say, and I see the
past eradicated like white lines drawn down the
center of a highway in lemon juice or invisible ink.
I hang up the phone, stumble back to this present,
this long letter of goodbye, this suicide note I'm
leaving for my life so that it can try to understand

where it lost me, where it went wrong in bringing me along.

And as I write these words I'm thinking of a bridge, the curve in it as it hooks towards and away from the place I used to live, where there was a girl I truly loved in the spiritual sense, who lived in the shadow of that bridge and wrote poetry, who enchanted me one summer as I was falling out of the bewitchment of another's spell; she is someone I hardly ever think of unless she calls me on the spiritual telephone, the line of which still runs between us. I sorrow at her having become a housewife married to a mechanic, and how our bodies never came together in the easy way our souls did; when she calls I answer, I always accept her calls without question. Every time she wonders about her life my phone rings.

I could pick up the receiver and call anyone. I call my mother. She is happy to hear from me and at last I begin to talk to her about the hardships of my childhood, and she understands and doesn't take it to heart when I tell her how lonely I felt and how it imbedded in me a feeling of perpetual loneliness that, every now and then, swallows me up, and is always with me in at least some small degree. You know, she says, I always thought you were putting up a front; every time I saw you, you looked weak and vulnerable, but your words were always full of confidence or else hard and steely, and I took it for inner toughness, though now I see I should have trusted my instincts and gone with what I saw. And this conversation is incredibly gratifying, it was the right call to make, giving birth to a reconciliation which enables me to somehow tunnel my way out of the past and break through into a present that is now being eased by a cool breeze.

Yet, truly, on the unruled page my writing rises and falls like the fate of great nations, and nothing stands resolved, surely no questions are answered. I listen to footsteps on the stairs, stopping one floor short of where I am, an occurrence that makes me happy, happy to be inside of writing, inside this room, inside this house that is inside a season that is now all snow and wind.

The world has fallen, snow blocking the streets, casting a spectral whiteness, a pallor on the fronts of houses, cutting off all passageways.

And now I am on a train, heading into New York City, except that I get off at Woodside in Queens, it is cold and snow is falling. I don't know my destination, for this is memory and memory is impure. It's cold, my breath becoming frost in air. I step out into snow; I am going nowhere; it was somewhere then, but now it is nowhere. Snow, wet as it melts upon my face. I begin walking through it; but here, knee-deep in snow, there isn't a path, I doubt I am ever getting through.

□

The long pilgrimage of thought
deposits me on the doorstep of Night.
Incredible the way minds work,
some to break through into enlightened realms,
others to lose themselves in dead ends.

I know there's a poem around here someplace,
lost in some unilluminated corner. People who

45

continually write about the same thing are either boring or, if they can write marvellously about their passion, are genius caught up in the throes of obsession.

Pardon me. I had no desire to go off
on this track. I was simply trying
to refuse the towline when the phone rang
and it wasn't for me.

☐

Yoga this morning, and a borrowed style. I spent 5 minutes staring at the sky, caught in a trance of blue. There is a season ending, and it seems so arbitrary, sculpted out of time, and yet we move from one day to the next, hardly pause to remember that we are officially
                    entering
                    winter.
The first day of it houses the longest night of the year, everything this experience has been moving towards. Yet it stands on the other side, like some first rite in the Egyptian mysteries.

The sun is pale in the sky, masked by clouds that even now are crackling with small imperceivable electrical charges. And now the sun breaks through and falls upon this page, Barbara sitting next to me, combing out her just washed hair. And now her combing begins to spray me with little droplets of water.

"Is Artie bringing anything?" she asks, a first utterance external to this monologue.

"I don't know," I say, in a voice that is vocal and real.

46

Combing briskly she bounces up and down on the bed, in her actions bouncing me, this book, this pen, only the sunlight is motionless, and it burns faintly now, though with faith and assurity.

☐

At times I believe she has abandoned me;
I feel empty, barren, like a pumpkin
scooped out to compose a face.
Those are the times I truly despair
and there is no one who can salvage me,
believing my life a shipwreck,
its hull ripped open
on the rocks of circumstance.

Hearing her voice beginning to murmur
close to my ear, I am revived,
regain hope, find the human energy
to be able to continue. And she,
invisible always, is the only one
who can cover the distance I find
between myself and the world;
she is not a dream but a presence,
and though I have never looked upon her face
she has held me gently in her arms,
calling me by the many names of love,
promising never to leave me
though always departing
the moment I begin to doubt her.

I can only believe, when she leaves,
that she means to return,
bringing to me a scent of life
that echoes flowers, her embrace

shielding me from
the endless emanations of death and decay,
illuminating a path that provides
a way out of existence as it is commonly known.

☐

With all my clothes on
I weight 140 pounds
on the scale of Pride.
I am ignorant, overabundant
in self-personality, desirous,
always prone to aversion and possessiveness.
Look at the way I treat what I write.
I act like I own it.

This is the book's last day.
Today its progress leaves me forever.

There is smoke rising
behind the buildings across the street,
their roofs covered with snow.

The phone rang three times.
I picked up the receiver.
There was no one on the line.

I wrote that down fast,
figuring whoever it was
would call back.
They didn't.

So much for that.

I could begin to talk about ignorance.

I don't really know anything about the eternal, only what I, at times, intuit, and my intuition may be as off-beam as a defective searchlight. All I know is that sometimes a perception pierces me like an arrow, and I have to groan or gasp and clutch at the part of my body where I have been struck: so often it seems to be my heart. And that leads me to think it is all delusion, emotion, and that it is actually the worldly striking home with the full force of its presence. So often out of the world, I misinterpret what is happening, dream I have finally broken through to a moment of grace.

What I took to be the purity of my visions was really a voice within, beginning to tell me how I could commit the crime of individualizing myself, thereby setting in motion the process of my separation from a divine state of bliss.

I have looked for the perfect and been endlessly disappointed, finding only a finite changing world and people who were troubled by as much confusion as I was. The Stoics said "Don't complain about your life. The door is always open if you wish to leave it." And that is wonderful, to see death as an open door, however false that notion may be.

Poetry has always been, for me, an open door, at least whenever it begins to happen; then I am able to walk through it either out of or into my life, depending upon where I'm starting from. And sometimes I think that, if I weren't blessed with the capability to traverse the different realms, I would surely die, for there would be no machinery for tapping back into the dynamo of life after having really exhausted myself.

For, in the writing of a poem, I'm sometimes

able to walk away from myself, shuck off person-
ality and walk naked into some realm where I am
no longer me; it is no longer my intelligence, the
instrument with which I look, that is in control,
but the actual Looker writing the words down,
peering into something the self, blind as a bat,
could never see. And, when I come back to myself,
I am refreshed, and there are words where a tree
might look, coming out of its trance, and see
leaves. Maybe

> these words are leaves, each a different
> shape, a different hue, though
> so often now I feel as if
> I am writing on a field of pure snow.

August 16 — December 20, 1977
Barton, Vermont — Montreal, Quebec

3

Acts
of the Imagination

Someday, in the great future, perhaps
there will be men
no longer torn,
for whom time is one eternal now
and change an ever-changing change,
who see the permanent in the impermanent
and the same rose in every dying rose.

Louis Dudek,
Atlantis

The slow, slow light in the winter sky
this very early morning assures us the world
is not the actual world. Never was.

William Bronk,
The Force of Desire

Disneyland will never be completed, as long as
there is imagination left in the world.

Walt Disney,
July 17, 1955

The Argument

Night is what we have always had,
day what we constantly fall back upon.

Who speaks for light? I do,
reincarnated into this life
to wield a sword that cuts through darkness.
I can transform my hands into a chalice,
my eyes into radiant suns.
Some mornings I can feel
my angelic wings beginning to unfold.

Poems as weapons,
creation an act effected
to entrap the Destructive Spirit.

Sacred words
can overwhelm the prince of demons,
drive him deep into unconsciousness.
While he lies undone in the dark
poems can be fashioned
in which to ensnare him, poems
to aid in the fight of good against evil,
to act as warriors
in the inevitable hand to hand combat
for the destiny of souls
in the cause of infinite divinity.

Night is what we have always had,
day what we constantly fall back upon.

I

I would have to be a fool to go on
being caught up in the poses of pain
(my foolishness, in the past, already proven);
I'm alive today,
sitting by a lake
while birds and crickets sing,
while the grass continues being green
and the waters of the lake flow into the beach
with calm and assurity.

First act of the imagination:
seeing the sun in yourself,
to decide to be alive,
freeing oneself from death-giving habits,
untying the soul from the body's
gravitational dominion, finding a way
to rise above the infinite gorge
that will cannibalize you, consume you whole
should you allow its star to ascend.

A different star comes to rest
in a distant constellation:
the star of your decision
to go on living, to take hold
of the reins. When pain cuts through you
it is only the body reacting
to what it knows best, the power
and pull of emotions.

There are flowers growing
wherever we stop to rest.
Today they are purple

with petals that are thin
and shoot out from an undramatic centre.

And yes, the sun's in the sky
though many clouds have gathered
in an attempt to veil its majesty,
but its golden light pours out into the air
and falls upon this page.

So much of what day gives
is stolen away by night
when we find it to be
dark and lonely and silent.
Suddenly awakening from sleep
we are in pieces
and each part is spinning
at its own speed.
Though we may attempt
to reconcile this disparate machinery
and the panicked overseers, our senses,
we should only accept
that the self is once again working
in mysterious ways.
And though night may seem dark and terrible
and the self caught up in war and conflict
it all eventually passes somehow
and we are spilled out onto
the early morning shores of light
where we are free to wander at our leisure,
meditate if we can, or else simply enjoy
the calming values of grass, wind, water and sun.

And now a barn roof in the distance
is aglow with sunlight and becomes

a silver mirror reflecting light back into the sky.
A seagull lazily flaps its wings
as it skirts across the top of the lake

(and somewhere in the near distance
the thundering, shattering sound
of breaking glass)
(and then the endless sweeping up
of small pieces, careful steps
made across a floor, and the awful worry
that comes in the wake of a broken window).

II

For months I've been staying
at the Hotel Unknown,
sleeping on orange sheets,
looking out at the world
through an orange window,
holding on tight to a blue blanket,
to an ideal vision of a blue world.

Who sends us off
on these wild and wicked tours
of the towns the damned inhabit?
Who plans the schedules
for these trips we take
through the underworld
unless it be that excellent
guide and world traveller
who once again has found himself
in the employ of Blake's Tours?

The price of passage

is always the act of loving.
We stand in the great hall
of the most holy temple
until, in a manipulated moment,
the floor drops away
and we are sent hurtling
into the awful subterranean darkness
where we travel by ferry
and broken foot-path
until the wailing starts,
only to finally be silenced
by the ultimate torture of ice.

But today we are far from that,
the hotel, for the moment,
left far behind;
we are, instead,
ushered into a world
of tap-dancing caterpillars,
grasshoppers with long red hind legs
and sailboats gliding idly through the watery blue.

It is the blue world
I have dreamed of, blue sky,
blue lake, blue hat
on my head, a blue
carpet as a welcome mat
and a life full of blue intentions.
Things are not sad or wistful
but only peaceful with a perfect naturalness.
Across the lake
there are waterfront pine forests
and off in other distances
red and white houses
worked beautifully into the landscape.

Life seen from this far away
takes on a pristine loveliness
until even things that are close to us
assume a divine beauty.

Young girls in bikinis
riding motorcycles
will become my lovers
in the next life,
the mermaid of this life
dying out. Even now
I don't know where she is;
she could be drowning in water,
she could be swimming in air,
she may be loving a worldly man
or burning her hair in celestial fire.

III

Imagination dies often
when the sun sets
and we are left to ponder
the greater secrets of the universe,
a universe we can't comprehend,
a universe bigger than the both of us.

Yet, although that view of the sky
overwhelms us with vast mystery,
we, too, are mysterious,
with little of our fullness called upon
by the non-demanding events
of the everyday.

Above all else

it is absolutely essential
to act as if this
is the only inhabited planet in the universe
and to recognize that each life
gracing this planet is unique,
will only pass here (or anywhere)
once, each form the vehicle
for its own private soul,
every soul a manifestation
of the essence that constitutes
all there is.

All mystical experience
resounds with the knowledge
of our being one being, and of
the one consciousness
existing in everything.
In the woods
I see myself in everything
but only in the sense
that every thing is part of everything else,
and all the world reverberates with echoes
of the one sound hidden behind the many.

There is joy in variation —
it's what makes life interesting —
but there is a higher, more refined joy
that comes from knowing
we are always at home
even as we wander down
the darker alleyways of life;
at all times we are tied into the one network
leading us back to the undivided state,
and what do we desire more
than lives that are illuminated?

IV

It is the hour of the beast,
the hour of the drowning lovers,
the hour when only my breath sings.

To have come this far
in the journey to oblivion
is to know both sides of the night
and to know you, my beloved,
as I'm afraid I know the book of the damned.

From what corner of the mind
does this originate?
The darkest corner
where nothing grows.
This, too, is imagination,
the mind's dark undertow
pulling us towards the dead
and what is dying.

To which pole,
the dark or the light,
would you have me set out?
I know you have said before
the light but

this is the hour we both stand in possession of the lie.

V

The dawn of first love over, completely over.
Yet it is not night that now enfolds you,
only the grey shadows of early morning.

The highway is waiting for you,
ready to take you wherever you might wish to go.
What's hardest and easiest:
deciding upon a destination,
somewhere the heart will be nourished
and unfold like a flower again.

VI

Awful dark boats
are out on the water tonight.
There's not a star in the sky,
water's black, sky's black
as engines of torment stir up
deep disturbing waters.
What horror to hear
the boats slipping out from the dock
on their journeys of evil intent.

To come this close to the edge
of the waters of oblivion,
to hear the boats setting out
and still be standing upon
a small square of the one true ground.
What if it all gave way
and you toppled headlong into the black,
what if you leaned out too far
over the side in morbid curiosity
to catch a glimpse of the faces
of those shadowy passengers
in the glow that exudes from dark?
What beings, stained with night,
drive the boats across chilling black waters
headed towards a horizon

where both sea and sky
meld into vast indistinguishable ink?

Across the water
small isolated lights
speak not of splendour
but of endurance,
telling of life on the other side
which we can get to
if only we can find the bridge.

Only the human mind can fathom
this much despair, create a world
in which fear rules and death
seeds every moment. The sky
filled with death angels,
the water seethes with demons,
even the ground is always prepared
to yawn wide and welcome you
into its cloying embrace.
And of fire it has been said
it is the sure way to damnation.

VII

Who will speak for the light?
A church stands outside my window
promising an afterlife
it may not be able to deliver.
But it is noble in its aspiration,
in its reaching for the upper limits of the sky,
and perhaps we can find heaven
by trying to climb up towards it
though, as experience teaches,

that may lead to a confusion of tongues.

Perhaps it is better
to sit with our spines contacting the earth
while elevating our consciousness
far beyond the upper limits of the sky,
letting it flow back into
what it has always known, letting
the seed it contains come to ground
to begin the process of growing and unfolding.
With simplicity I can say
there is an essence all things contain
that is like water poured out from the same well
originating from the same source
where two holy rivers meet.

The struggle is always
to get beyond suffering;
it keeps us from crossing thresholds,
keeps the heart encapsulated
and all of that radiant energy
becomes prisoner and languishes
deep within the cell where it has been confined.
Hours of torment teach us
what hell is and why we must not choose it.

VIII

Inspiration may hinge
upon the influence of a star;
from the mountaintop
all the world appears to be shimmering
while down below
fields are plotted out in green.

And there are times
when everything gets too organized
and the mind flounders,
for it can easily take to
the clear and easy walkways
and forget about pioneering
any new territory.
Like all other things
it follows the path of least resistance,
and like the heart
will radiate outwards
only when totally unthreatened.

We talk so much about holiness
yet there is nothing sacred about us
as we sit in uncomfortable chairs,
reemphasizing the awkwardness
of our shared life.
We both want purity
yet, by our actions, work
to undermine all innocence.

IX

Imagination: the seat of pain,
well-spring of suffering.
We have allowed it to work this way
far too long, and we
have crippled ourselves
simply by believing it is so.
No pain greater
than that of the mind,
manacles fashioned out of anguish and fear,

and, knowing this, one day
we will push off from pain
like Ulysses from Circe's island,
never to return, on our way at last
back to the faithful one
we have always truly loved.

X

Rain is falling
upon fields of clover and wheat and oats
and in the sandy marram grass
a couple is making love
while the potential
for thousands of magic mushrooms
floats about in the air.
Where, yesterday, we walked
on the beach at last, trying
to reconcile the differences
between man and woman for all time,
today there are small uncategorized
green plants sprouting up
in the impressions
our passing feet have made.

A woman stands before me
with tears in her eyes
and they are tears of pain and indignation.
Yet deep within the earth
the word is out:
everything is beginning to change.
Soon everyone will look like everyone else
and we will all walk along beaches

chanting as one voice
for whatever it is that will finally fulfill us
to come from across the water.

We walked as the sky began to change
from blue to deeper blue
and talked as soul mates
of all the trials and joys of the journey.
Would we be reconciled at last?
It seemed so, though of course
in the hours after
it all faded,
an insubstantial dream.

When voices shout loud enough
they hammer at the doorway of the heart
and force it open, and when the moment
is one of intimacy the heart rushes
to throw open its windows
to let in the light, to let its own light out.
Above all we must be gentle,
for that is all that ensures
the process will continue, the heart stay open
and life be given a chance to renew itself.

Romantic visions
transform everything into paradise,
and that is why we must never forget
sorrow and misunderstanding, all things
the mind attempts to conquer
with the force of will, leading to
an act of the imagination
that lies as it unveils itself.

XI

We must take time out here
for the poet's life has reached
the beautiful poem level
in which he is not writing down
words that attempt to be poetic
but rather is living inside instants
in which all the poetry in life
is flooding in at his senses.
As clouds go drifting by
over the majestic hills,
so awe-inspiring as to be indescribable,
he knows what poetry is,
knows that his life,
at least for the moment,
is poetically perfect.

And it is only coincidence
that changes the mood, gets things
moving along an entirely different track.
The numinous yields to conversation
and we discover coincidence
takes us back inside time
in a moment that ignites with strange collision
but surely one that brings things
into focus rather than letting the mind
drift like clouds across the sky.
Magic fades into obscurity
and with magic poetry fades,
the hills are just hills again,
not even what they truly are
but just the mind seeing *hills*.

XII

The sky overcast,
a band of light on the horizon,
the waves of the sea tempestuous
when we come to meet again.
We talk little
but study the rocks, the waves, the seaweed.
It is no bright morning;
we are headed for dark night
but, for the moment, the sea in its uproar
will suffice. Always the sea,
we are always by the sea
when meeting or parting.
Only when I am alone
do I see the wind flowing
over the earth like water.

Coming to meet, always,
you in your many disguises,
I eternally the small shell of self
you have always known,
we walk the beaches,
sometimes talking of the vestments
we have assumed, other times
discussing phenomenology.
There are still points, of course,
moments I am completely satisfied
when your divinity is seen.
Too often I am mistaking you
for something I can have,
something I have always wanted,
rather than seeing you are the beautiful given.

XIII

The sun burns brightly in the sky
and it is a morning that could go on forever,
clouds perfuming the hills,
the early morning sound of traffic,
and off in the distance
the sound of the sea,
the one sound always hidden behind the many.

At last we are standing
among the evergreens,
and we have become so peaceful,
so gentle, so rooted
that birds alight upon us
and, in a moment, begin to sing.

Bright morning
after dark dark nights,
nights confused by the power of the mind,
nights staggered by the heart's desire for love.
We walk out into morning tired but radiant,
sit humbly like sunflowers
bowing their heads beneath the light of the sun.

The self is in its element,
has surrounded itself at last
with life breath, air
the element in which we move
that sustains us, swirls around us,
carries us as the water does each little fish.
Surely we listen to a speaking wind
in the hours that follow dawn,
and what it tells us gives us strength
to continue wanting to live forever.

Grass still damp
with morning dew, and the air
filled with the sound of human voices.
Who is talking to who?
There are voices that file reports
while others simply whisper
soft words of comfort
to those who have spent far too long sorrowing
over the severing of bonds that were never secure.

XIV

And there is no assurance
the Holocaust will never be repeated
and we could linger upon
the viciousness of perverse and necrophilic men,
and we ourselves could become too attached
to the dead who have been buried
and, in so doing, make it even easier
for it all to happen again.
Everything in existence tells us
to strive for a new world
in which life will be worshipped,
to leave graves and cold stone
as monuments of the past,
reminders of what once occurred
but never as what we place
in the future before us.
For surely, in these forms,
we will die, but that is one story,
one well of reconciliation,
and yet each sees the living taking place
as something different,
and there is no formula for beauty

(although invoking pastoral images
is always good for a start),
and where the poets have failed
is in having desired to be canonized
in the palace of art
when all along they should have been striving
for integrity rather than an influential position at court
or a good spot in the museum of artifacts.
They should have been aspiring
to become souls that are powered upwards,
that break free at last when the body
falls back to the earth that constitutes it.

XV

A man who comes to the sea
with an open heart
must surely find inspiration,
and if his Muse, the moon,
is in the sky all the better.
He hears the shifting sound of waves
and the soft lull that rocks beneath,
the frantic sound of a boat engine
starting up and faltering in the distance.
He is looking east and there is
a pink tinge that forms a line across the sky,
moon almost full, boat
almost started, and he sits alone
quite peacefully on the cold sand
and writes these words to say
his heart is with you now.

You stand on a bridge
looking down into a flowing stream

and see your feelings
are just like the stream
as its essence stays
and the flowing goes on forever.
Perhaps it will run out at the source someday
but for now it is with you
and there are bridges across
which you can use whenever you need to
and you know that whenever you feel the desire
you can put your hand
into the essence,
draw a handful up to your lips
and drink down the cool, satisfying element.

The moon is hanging
in a field of purple
that is what the sky has become,
and no one else will ever see it
exactly in the way you're seeing it now
for each mind is unique
and every eye focuses differently.
Some days it's beautiful to be alive
and you are, full of the knowledge
that you can experience the eternal
if only you allow your whole being
to experience right now.
And any fears you might have
are assuaged by the vision
of a lighthouse stationed at a distant point,
its beacon prepared to radiate light
in the face of all disasters.

Behind you the lights of the town
come on one by one
and form a chain of light

that will shine in the dark
just as the stars will shine in the sky
a short time from this moment
we are now inhabiting together.
The air is cooling
and yet the lights of the town shine,
are reflected on the surface of the water.
The ocean is peaceful tonight,
there's not a cloud in the sky,
nature has perfected itself
in a moment that is occupying your senses,
and you have become the perfect lens
for the world to look through
in order to be able to see itself.

Montreal, Quebec — Neil Harbour,
Cape Breton
Summer 1979

4

Clouds:
A Sequence of Days

There, somewhere, at the horizon
           you cannot tell the sea from the sky,
where the white cloud glimmers,

the only reality, in a sea of unreality,

out of that cloud come palaces, and domes,
                    and marble capitals,
and carvings of ivory and gold —
                    Atlantis
shines invisible, in that eternal cloud.

Louis Dudek
Atlantis

come home to heaven
thru a gate of clouds

bp Nichol
The Martyrology, Book 2

sequence of days

jagged horizon
always looming at the edge of the blue
only a trace of light
casting its cover from a window

in the distance
jets descending to dorval
in landing patterns, while here

light falls, snow
over the world, soft yellow
in the night, by day white-hot

☐

glad it changes, day to day
pain pulling back
nova scotia fog
obscured the coastline for 5 days

we camped in among the trees
I walked daily down to the edge of the water
to see no more than twenty feet out
sat in isolation / separation
a wall of silence between us

getting over first love
trying to

I thought we would kill each other in that tent
hard demands flying both ways

shitting in the woods
found poisonous red-capped amanita

poison that is always there

I kept wondering if they were hallucinogenic

I read of them
in Graves' *Greek Myths*
and then they appeared

what we think we want can kill us

☐

cold night, wasted day

the taste of tea and cloves
honey to sweeten what it can

frustrations stretching on past arm's length

neat and organized on the page:
this expression of categorized pain

☐

suffering in style
not dying hungry in the streets of Calcutta

one out of three children in the world
starving to death before the age of five

seeing it on the news
I break into tears

though it is myself
I cry for

☐

sky full of clouds
breaking apart
to let through the blue

last night snow fell
after love making

this morning:
snow swirling in the wind

☐

the stars in Orion's belt
so bright tonight

the sky dark, deep blue
with heartbreak

frost on the windows

listening to mice
scampering in the walls

my voice
singing in air,
sad love song, a lament of possibilities

high overhead: moon
that will meet the rosy dawn
morning beginning in its billion year fashion

burning at both ends

☐

we dance under that north star
having pulled away from the city
having taken to the air
to see what can be discovered

how much of what was Atlantis
has become the sky, the clouds,
this deep blue we now pass through?

the old voyage of discovery
took us across seas
we followed Columbus
across mysterious oceans

but now here we are in air
and there is that sense
of the intangible,
we do not feel at home here

this is what we have progressed to:
this voyage through the invisible
with only light as our guide
with only light to tell us
see this as blue, this as dark

we always wanted the sky
and now we have it
but what is it?

the realm of our thinking
the mind we aspired to

and freedom, why else
desire wings to fly like a bird?

what holds us here in air?

manipulated currents
the way we have learned to master them

these clouds barely buffet us

we move in and out of them freely,
insubstantial islands of cloud
that dare us to step out onto them

they suggest there's a place for us
in the sky, that we can build upon clouds,
walk upon them, that we can live in mid-air

☐

haven't seen any angels yet
nor any flying saucers

tonight it seems
the only intelligent life up here
is us

☐

another coastline

the end of january

golden full moon shrouded by cloud
shining down upon vancouver

standing on a pier
looking out over the water
golden moonlight shining in the watery silver

anchored tankers
mountains across the inlet
barely tinged by snow

our most romantic moments
are so often spent alone
the whole world unfolding

the gulls / the moon / the ships / the city

□

mountains
covered with snow
rivers floating rafts of ice
the movement onward
continuing

thoughts of you
becoming the miles behind

as the bus starts climbing
up into the mountains
it begins to snow

the long voyage out
ending a cycle
putting distance
between the two shores of my life
letting water flow between

winter constricts
confines
the rivers are bound up
trees endure and tell nothing
snow falls and falls
all around me
mountains squeezing in against the road

☐

what I want is sleep
what I get is poetry

maybe

the poetry of words

began this bus ride
before it was light
rode across mountain roads all through the day
now it's night
and I'm still riding

how much is it worth to you?
is the question everything now asks

☐

the days a haze of geography
mountains, trees, the rugged terrain
of the b.c. interior,
the abject ugliness of prince george

sitting on a bus
on my way back to vancouver

here in a tentative valley
between mountains
the pressure in my head
in constant flux
as we rise and fall
from rocky heights

I feel
we've entered the badlands
slag heap mountains
a scarcity of trees
the landscape cries privation
though, writing that,
I look up
as we bridge across
a beautiful river
now following the road

the river lined with ice
waters teeming

fog crashing down on the rim of the mountain

behind me
a child speaking in a foreign language

ahead somewhere
Hell's Gate

Creeley quoted Olson
on art being life's only twin

the sky a delta
between the mountains

will the chinese come and get us
or leave us here to die alone?

river snaking through the mountains
railway line following the river
deliberately, set there
with a plan in mind

phenomena

even the sudden white water
the power line poles
with their 4 horizontal bars

overlapping crucifixions
the river lined with ice and stone

approaching Hell's Gate
and beyond it
the little town of Hope

☐

ships at anchorage
fog veiling the mountains
across english bay

a girl whistling and kissing
for her dog
engine noise
flooding in from the distance

sitting on the pier again
air cold
birds in flight overhead

this strange winter voyage
and a poem being written
while a buoy sounds
like an oboe tuning

ships
sitting in the bay
landmarks to some drifting emotion

joey
you are drowned in these waters

going to the planetarium now
I'll look for you / I'll find you
among the stars

☐

southern california

storm after storm
assaults these coastlines
and the ground can't absorb the rain

hills fall
mudslides come crashing down
onto the pacific coast highway
houses are crushed
by rushing torrents of rain and mud

the tv always on
always reporting
the latest disasters
the next storm that's coming in

I remember the love
that's still dying out

who knows what will be left
after the rain

☐

I love Suzanne when she's drunk or stoned
or even when she's sleepy
tired-eyed, running her fingers through her hair

her eyes and the pacific
merging into the blue
I'll always see before me

I keep loving Barbara
from these distances
across the wall of marriage

two women
standing behind the gates
the past / the present

always I'm the man left standing
on the other side
either waving goodbye
or else trying to lure the mare
out beyond her securing fences

look for me on the horizon
turning matter into light

□

standing at the end of santa monica pier
the sun reflecting off the water
blinded by the light

pier's end
looking out onto the pacific

is Beatrice the end, the way
or only the beauty that graces the voyage?

□

a plateau of cloud

sun streaming in the plane window
the sky divided
white below / blue above
a white horizon line
seen in the distance

no world below
only cloud
no stars above
only blue
deepening into blue forever

□

the clouds get mountainous

no longer a flat plain
they jut up into the blue

there's a cabin on a hill
made out of the whiteness of cloud
this a strange lifeless land
where nothing lives
but what the mind imagines

if only we could be freed
of our imperfections, gross matter
that anchors us to earth

here we could be as angels
or as gods
reclining in bowers of cumulus
or surfing on an ocean of billowing cloud
the untainted sky
hovering above us

jet liners take off for these heights
and disappear
never to be seen again
they find an entryway
into a perfect world
their fuel transforms
and suddenly they have the power
to hover at these heights forever

☐

the sun's mirror image
burning in the clouds below
the sun above casting light
in through this window

and the image below,

reflected not in water but in cloud,
burning into my eyes

☐

first came the winter of my discontent
then the fall from grace and gracefulness
when I stumbled over the word *failure*
which lay upon the ground like a fallen tree

in summer I journeyed
until, for a moment,
I became the grail, that crystal chalice

what lies ahead, what disguises,
what woman mistaken for a boy?

in the sunlight of afternoon
I begin to see
all transformed to comedy

as the eye that frames the seen
dollies back to reveal
gods in the heavens
supplying trial for those they most love

☐

these human failings

how can we even attempt immortal art
when we fail one another
in such obvious ways
daily

☐

But fare ye well, 'tis partly my own fault,
Which death, our absence, soon shall remedy.

always the shadow of the gallows
falls upon the ground of comedy

if there is a world of light the world of dark will appear
                                                    below
perhaps with souls in torment, perhaps emptied forever
of all human presence, but surely going on
for as long as heaven goes on, the night outside the mead hall

what isn't my fault, my interpretation?

and it is the world I live in, waiting for a principle of
                                                    balance
to manifest within it and grow like a seed
into something beautiful and unthought of,
something I could never anticipate,
the beauty of a life
achieving fullness in its time

☐

They are fairies, he who speaks to them shall die.

the beautiful appearances, presences
always with us, living in the grass beneath our feet,
spiriting the wind and air
with their magical lives

we call them sprites,
creatures of air, lovely Ariel
a sea nymph in his latest guise
though it is perhaps Puck

Goblin, lead them up and down!

☐

do we dare talk with the fairies
or only watch silently as they manifest?

I once shook hands with a leprechaun
he laughed
it was not the touch of death

who can distinguish our visions from the real?
who are we to contradict what the heart knows?

☐

each journey has its language, its conditions
this journey I go through alone

in the fall I could still see her there
at a distance, but there
I could see the tracing of her footsteps in the snow

then separation
the journey out
into a transformed and transforming world

it's the world
I want to embrace
and a real love who is of that world

there is the day
in all of its intensity, its onlyness
one day and one life

□

we stand in shadow
as the millennium unfolds
can only pray
those who wield the power
that could destroy it all
know restraint, know compassion
and see the future of humankind
as the essence of every dream

□

what we make out of what we've felt
I guess that becomes art

it must be said
without placing what *is* said upon a pedestal
bring art down into the street
see if it survives

most art a limited perfection
like the sky with its clouds
beautiful
but we can't live there

we want inhabitable places

this life we live
to shine through in our language

bring it down,
force the poet to come down from his clouds,
seed the clouds
and watch as poetry falls as rain

□

returned to this corner of the world
hungry for food
hungry for love

long past spring's beginning
almost at its end

I open the balcony door
focus my eyes on the sky's
imaginable light

passing before the sun:
planes, clouds, a sequence of days
the only mimesis

the sky an openness

though we can't live there
we take flight
from time to time

standing now on the ground
feeling the desire for life

give up on death's sweet oblivion
hold fast to life
take in the light

and let the small precious flame of the heart
be seen.

Montreal — Vancouver — Los Angeles —
Vancouver — Montreal
Jan. 2-June 11, 1980

By the Same Author

Vegetables (1975)
Under the Skin (1976)
Report on the Second Half of the Twentieth Century (1977)
Proverbsi (with Tom Konyves) (1977)
Montreal English Poetry of the Seventies (ed. with
    Endre Farkas, 1977)
The Perfect Accident (1978)
The Book of Fall (1979)
Autokinesis (1980)
To Sleep, To Love (1982)
Eight Odes (1982)
Cross/cut: Contemporary English Quebec Poetry
    (ed. with Peter Van Toorn, 1982)
The Insecurity of Art (ed. with Peter Van Toorn, 1982)
Acts of the Imagination (1983)
Whirlwinds (1983)
The Better Part of Heaven (1984)
Canadian Poetry Now (ed., 1984)
The Little Magazine in Canada 1925-80 (1984)
One Night (1985)
In the Spirit of the Times (1986)
Islands (1986)